table of
contents

classic sweets

Individual Tiramisu Cups

Makes 2 servings

 4 whole ladyfingers, torn into bite-size pieces
 6 tablespoons cold strong coffee *or* ⅓ cup water
     and ½ teaspoon instant coffee granules (mixed
     together until dissolved)
 2 packets sugar substitute
 ½ teaspoon vanilla
 ½ cup thawed fat-free whipped topping
 1½ teaspoons cocoa powder
 1 tablespoon sliced almonds

1. Place half of lady finger pieces in each of two 6-ounce pyrex dishes. Set aside.

2. Combine coffee, sugar substitute and vanilla in small bowl. Stir until sugar substitute is dissolved. Spoon 3 tablespoons of coffee mixture over each serving of ladyfinger pieces.

3. Place whipped topping in small bowl. Fold in cocoa until blended. Spoon topping over each dessert. Cover with plastic wrap and refrigerate at least 2 hours.

4. Meanwhile, place small skillet over medium-high heat until hot. Add almonds and toast 2 to 3 minutes or until golden brown, stirring constantly. Remove from heat.

5. Sprinkle toasted almonds over each dessert before serving.

Nutrients per serving: 1 Tiramisu Cup
Calories: 148, **Calories from Fat:** 30%, **Total Fat:** 5g,
Saturated Fat: 1g, **Cholesterol:** 80mg, **Sodium:** 43mg,
Carbohydrate: 22g, **Fiber:** 1g, **Protein:** 4g

Dietary Exchange: 1½ Starch, 1 Fat

Chocolate Flan

Makes 8 servings

- 2 **eggs, lightly beaten**
- 24 **packets NatraTaste® Brand Sugar Substitute**
- 2 **heaping tablespoons unsweetened cocoa powder**
- 1 **tablespoon cornstarch**
- 1 **teaspoon almond extract**
- 1 **(15-ounce) can evaporated skim milk**
- 1 **cup fat-free milk**

1. Preheat oven to 350°F. Coat a 3-cup mold with nonstick cooking spray.

2. In a medium bowl, whisk together eggs, NatraTaste®, cocoa, cornstarch and almond extract until smooth. Stir in evaporated milk and fat-free milk. Pour mixture into mold. Place mold in a baking pan filled halfway with water.*

3. Bake 2 hours. Mixture will not look completely set, but will become firm upon cooling. Let cool at room temperature 1 hour, then refrigerate for several hours. To serve, invert mold onto a plate, or spoon flan from the mold.

*Baking mold in water bath helps cook the flan evenly without cracking.

Nutrients per serving: ⅛ of total recipe
Calories: 82, **Calories from Fat:** 22%, **Total Fat:** 2g,
Saturated Fat: 2g **Cholesterol:** 56mg, **Sodium:** 93mg,
Carbohydrate: 13g, **Fiber:** <1g, **Protein:** 7g

Dietary Exchange: 1½ Starch, ½ Milk

Apricot Dessert Soufflé

Makes 6 servings

- **3 tablespoons butter**
- **2 tablespoons all-purpose flour**
- **1 cup no-sugar-added apricot pourable fruit***
- **⅓ cup finely chopped dried apricots**
- **3 egg yolks, beaten**
- **4 egg whites**
- **¼ teaspoon cream of tartar**
- **⅛ teaspoon salt**

*¾ cup no-sugar-added fruit spread mixed with ¼ cup warm water can be substituted.

Preheat oven to 325°F. Melt butter in medium saucepan. Add flour; cook, stirring constantly, until bubbly. Add pourable fruit and apricots; cook, stirring constantly, until thickened, about 3 minutes. Remove from heat; blend in egg yolks. Cool to room temperature, stirring occasionally. Beat egg whites with cream of tartar and salt in small bowl with electric mixer at high speed until stiff peaks form. Gently fold into apricot mixture. Spoon into 1½-quart soufflé dish. Bake 30 minutes or until puffed and golden brown.** Garnish as desired. Serve immediately.

**Soufflé will be soft in center. For a firmer soufflé, increase baking time to 35 minutes.

Nutrients per serving: ⅙ of total recipe
Calories: 148, **Calories from Fat:** 53%, **Total Fat:** 9g,
Saturated Fat: 5g, **Cholesterol:** 123mg, **Sodium:** 151mg,
Carbohydrate: 14g, **Fiber:** 1g, **Protein:** 4g

Dietary Exchange: 1 Fruit, ½ Meat, 1½ Fat

Lemon Mousse Squares

Makes 9 servings

> 1 cup graham cracker crumbs
> 2 tablespoons reduced-fat margarine, melted
> 1 packet sugar substitute *or* equivalent of
>   2 teaspoons sugar
> ⅓ cup cold water
> 1 packet unflavored gelatin
> 2 eggs, well beaten
> ½ cup lemon juice
> ¼ cup sugar
> 2 teaspoon grated lemon peel
> 2 cups thawed fat-free whipped topping
> 1 container (8 ounces) lemon-flavored sugar-free,
>   fat-free yogurt

1. Spray 9-inch square baking pan with nonstick cooking spray. Stir together graham cracker crumbs, margarine and sugar substitute in small bowl. Press into bottom of prepared pan with fork; set aside.

2. Combine cold water and gelatin in small microwavable bowl; let stand 2 minutes. Microwave at HIGH 40 seconds to dissolve gelatin; set aside.

3. Combine eggs, lemon juice, sugar and lemon peel in top of double boiler. Cook, stirring constantly, over boiling water, about 4 minutes or until thickened. Remove from heat; stir in gelatin mixture. Refrigerate about 25 minutes or until mixture is thoroughly cooled and begins to set.

4. Gently combine cooled gelatin mixture, whipped topping and yogurt. Pour into prepared crust. Refrigerate 1 hour or until firm. Cut into 9 squares before serving.

Nutrients per serving: 1 Square (⅑ of total recipe)
Calories: 154, **Calories from Fat:** 29%, **Total Fat:** 5g,
Saturated Fat: 1g, **Cholesterol:** 47mg, **Sodium:** 124mg,
Carbohydrate: 24g, **Fiber:** 1g, **Protein:** 3g

Dietary Exchange: 1½ Starch, 1 Fat

classic **sweets**

Quick Chocolate Pudding

Makes 4 servings

- ¼ **cup unsweetened cocoa powder**
- 2 **tablespoons cornstarch**
- 1½ **cups reduced-fat (2%) milk**
- 6 **to 8 packets sugar substitute** *or* **equivalent of ⅓ cup sugar**
- 1 **teaspoon vanilla**
- ⅛ **teaspoon ground cinnamon (optional)**
- **Assorted sugar-free candies (optional)**

MICROWAVE DIRECTIONS

1. Combine cocoa powder and cornstarch in medium microwavable bowl or 1-quart glass measure. Gradually whisk in milk until well blended.

2. Microwave at HIGH 2 minutes; stir. Microwave at MEDIUM-HIGH (70% power) 3 to 4½ minutes or until thickened, stirring every 1½ minutes.

3. Stir in sugar substitute, vanilla and cinnamon, if desired. Let stand at least 5 minutes before serving, stirring occasionally to prevent skin from forming. Serve warm or chilled. Garnish with candies just before serving, if desired.

Nutrients per serving: ⅓ cup pudding (without candy garnish)
Calories: 78, **Calories from Fat:** 23%, **Total Fat:** 2g,
Saturated Fat: 1g, **Cholesterol:** 7mg, **Sodium:** 56mg,
Carbohydrate: 10g, **Fiber:** <1g, **Protein:** 5g

Dietary Exchange: ½ Milk, ½ Fat

Rhubarb and Apple Crumble

Makes 6 servings

   3 cups peeled, cored, ¾-inch cubed Granny Smith apples
2½ cups ¾-inch cubed fresh red rhubarb
  ½ cup EQUAL® SPOONFUL*
  2 tablespoons cornstarch
  ⅓ cup water or apple juice
  1 tablespoon lemon juice
  1 teaspoon grated lemon peel (optional)

TOPPING
  ¾ cup quick or old-fashioned oats, uncooked
  ¼ cup raisins
  ¼ cup chopped nuts
  ⅓ cup EQUAL® SPOONFUL**
  2 tablespoons stick butter or margarine, melted
  ½ to ¾ teaspoon ground cinnamon
    Frozen yogurt, ice cream or whipped topping (optional)

*May substitute 12 packets EQUAL® sweetener.

**May substitute 8 packets EQUAL® sweetener.

• Combine apples, rhubarb, ½ cup Equal® and cornstarch. Place in 1½-quart casserole dish.

• Combine water, lemon juice and lemon peel. Pour over fruit mixture. Cover and bake in preheated 400°F oven 20 to 25 minutes or until fruit is tender.

• Meanwhile, combine oats, raisins, nuts, ⅓ cup Equal®, melted butter and cinnamon until well blended. Remove cover from fruit. Sprinkle with oats mixture.

• Return to oven and bake, uncovered, an additional 8 to 10 minutes or until topping is crisp. Serve warm with frozen yogurt, ice cream or whipped topping, if desired.

Nutrients per serving: ⅙ of total recipe
Calories: 177, **Calories from fat:** 41% **Total Fat:** 8g,
Cholesterol: 10mg, **Sodium:** 45mg, **Carbohydrate:** 26g,
Protein: 3g

Dietary Exchange: 1 Starch, 1 Fruit, 1½ Fat

classic sweets

Almond-Pumpkin Chiffon Pudding

Makes 8 servings

- **1 envelope unflavored gelatin**
- **1 cup 2% low-fat milk**
- **1 cup solid pack pumpkin**
- **½ teaspoon pumpkin pie spice**
- **1 container (8 ounces) plain low fat yogurt**
- **3 egg whites**
- **Dash salt**
- **⅔ cup packed brown sugar**
- **½ cup chopped roasted California Almonds, divided**

Sprinkle gelatin over milk in small saucepan; let stand 5 minutes to soften. Cook and stir constantly over low heat until gelatin dissolves; remove from heat. Stir in pumpkin and pumpkin pie spice. Cool to room temperature; stir in yogurt. Refrigerate until mixture begins to thicken and gel. Beat egg whites with salt to form soft peaks. Gradually beat in brown sugar, beating to form stiff peaks; fold into pumpkin mixture. Sprinkle 1 tablespoon almonds over bottom of greased 6-cup mold. Fold remaining almonds into pumpkin mixture; spoon into mold. Refrigerate until firm. Unmold to serve.

*Favorite recipe from **Almond Board of California***

Nutrients per serving: ⅛ of total recipe
Calories: 170, **Calories from Fat:** 27%, **Total Fat:** 5g,
Saturated Fat: 1g, **Cholesterol:** 4mg, **Sodium:** 65mg,
Carbohydrate: 25g, **Fiber:** 1g, **Protein:** 7g

Dietary Exchange: 1½ Starch, ½ Milk, ½ Fat

Blueberry Dream Fritters

Makes 12 fritters

>   **Vegetable oil**
> ½ **cup whipping cream**
> 1 **egg**
> 1 **teaspoon vanilla**
> 1 **cup self-rising flour**
> ⅓ **cup self-rising cornmeal**
> ⅓ **cup granulated sugar**
> 1½ **cups fresh blueberries**
>   **Powdered sugar**

1. Heat 2 inches oil in large heavy skillet to 375°F on deep-fat thermometer.

2. Meanwhile, combine cream, egg and vanilla in small bowl.

3. Combine flour, cornmeal and granulated sugar in large bowl. Stir in cream mixture just until moistened. Fold in blueberries.

4. Carefully drop batter by heaping tablespoonfuls into hot oil. Fry until golden brown, turning once. Drain well on paper towels. Sprinkle with powdered sugar; serve immediately.

Prep and Cook Time: 20 minutes

Nutrients per serving: 1 fritter
Calories: 110, **Calories from Fat:** 33%, **Total Fat:** 4g,
Cholesterol: 31mg, **Sodium:** 143mg, **Carbohydrate:** 16g,
Fiber: 1g, **Protein:** 2g

Dietary Exchange: 1 Starch, 1 Fat

Blueberry Dream Fritters

Mint Chocolate Cups

Makes 6 servings

    2 boxes (3 ounces total) sugar-free chocolate
      pudding mix
 2½ cups fat-free half-and-half
  ½ cup fat-free sour cream
    1 teaspoon vanilla
  ½ to 1 teaspoon peppermint extract
 1½ cups fat-free whipped topping
    6 sugar-free peppermint patties, chopped

1. In medium bowl, whisk pudding mix with half-and-half. Blend prepared pudding with sour cream, vanilla and peppermint extract until smooth.

2. Divide mixture evenly into 6 parfait glasses or dessert cups, with 2 tablespoons whipped topping in between to make layers. Top each with additional 2 tablespoons whipped topping. Chill 1 hour or until completely cold. Garnish each serving with 1 chopped peppermint patty.

Nutrients per serving: ⅔ cup chocolate mixture with ¼ cup whipped topping
Calories: 166, **Calories from Fat:** <1%, **Total Fat:** <1g,
Saturated Fat: <1g **Cholesterol:** 15mg, **Sodium:** 541mg,
Carbohydrate: 29g, **Fiber:** <1g, **Protein:** 6g

Dietary Exchange: 2 Starch

Mint Chocolate Cups

cookies, brownies & bars

Chocolate Orange Meringues

Makes 5 dozen cookies

- **3 egg whites**
- **½ teaspoon vanilla extract**
- **⅛ teaspoon orange extract**
- **¾ cup sugar**
- **¼ cup HERSHEY'®S Cocoa**
- **½ teaspoon freshly grated orange peel**

1. Heat oven to 300°F. Cover cookie sheet with parchment paper or foil.

2. Beat egg whites, vanilla and orange extract in large bowl on high speed of mixer until soft peaks form. Gradually add sugar, beating well after each addition until stiff peaks hold their shape, sugar is dissolved and mixture is glossy. Sprinkle half of cocoa and all of orange peel over egg white mixture; gently fold in just until combined. Repeat with remaining cocoa.

3. Spoon mixture into pastry bag fitted with large star tip; pipe 1½-inch-diameter stars onto prepared cookie sheet.

4. Bake 35 to 40 minutes or until dry. Cool slightly; peel paper from cookies. Cool completely on wire rack. Store, covered, at room temperature.

Nutrients per serving: 3 cookies
Calories: 35, **Calories from Fat:** 3%, **Total Fat:** <1g,
Sodium: 8mg, **Carbohydrate:** 8g, **Fiber:** <1g, **Protein:** 1g

Dietary Exchange: ½ Starch

Chocolate Peanut Butter Ice Cream Sandwiches

Makes 4 servings

> 2 tablespoons creamy peanut butter
> 8 chocolate wafer cookies
> ⅔ cup no-sugar-added vanilla ice cream, softened

1. Spread peanut butter over flat sides of all cookies.

2. Spoon ice cream over peanut butter on 4 cookies. Top with remaining 4 cookies, peanut butter sides down. Press down lightly to force ice cream to edges of sandwich.

3. Wrap each sandwich in foil; seal tightly. Freeze at least 2 hours or up to 5 days.

Nutrients per serving: 1 sandwich
Calories: 129, **Calories from Fat:** 49%, **Total Fat:** 7g,
Saturated Fat: 3g, **Cholesterol:** 4mg, **Sodium:** 124mg,
Carbohydrate: 15g, **Fiber:** 1g, **Protein:** 4g

Dietary Exchange: 1 Starch, 1 Fat

Chocolate Peanut Butter Ice Cream Sandwiches

Chocolate Chip Cookies

Makes about 2 dozen cookies

- ⅓ **cup stick butter or margarine, softened**
- 1 **egg**
- 1 **teaspoon vanilla**
- ⅓ **cup EQUAL® SPOONFUL***
- ⅓ **cup firmly packed light brown sugar**
- ¾ **cup all-purpose flour**
- ½ **teaspoon baking soda**
- ¼ **teaspoon salt**
- ½ **cup semi-sweet chocolate chips or mini chocolate chips**

*May substitute 8 packets EQUAL® sweetener.

• Beat butter with electric mixer until fluffy. Beat in egg and vanilla until blended. Mix in Equal® Spoonful and brown sugar until combined.

• Combine flour, baking soda and salt. Mix into butter mixture until well blended. Stir in chocolate chips.

• Drop dough by rounded teaspoonfuls onto ungreased baking sheet. Bake in preheated 350°F oven 8 to 10 minutes or until light golden color. Remove from baking sheet and cool completely on wire rack.

Nutrients per serving: 1 cookie
Calories: 70, **Calories from Fat:** 51%, **Total Fat:** 4g,
Saturated Fat: 2g, **Cholesterol:** 16mg, **Sodium:** 74mg,
Carbohydrate: 9g, **Fiber:** <1g, **Protein:** 1g

Dietary Exchange: ½ Starch, 1 Fat

Cinnamon Flats

Makes 50 cookies

1¾ **cups all-purpose flour**
½ **cup sugar**
1½ **teaspoons ground cinnamon**
¼ **teaspoon salt**
¼ **teaspoon ground nutmeg**
½ **cup (1 stick) cold margarine, cut into pieces**
3 **egg whites, divided**
1 **teaspoon vanilla**
1 **teaspoon water**
 Sugar Glaze (recipe follows)

1. Preheat oven to 350°F. Combine flour, sugar, cinnamon, salt and nutmeg in medium bowl. Cut in margarine with pastry blender or two knives until mixture forms coarse crumbs. Beat in 2 egg whites and vanilla, forming crumbly mixture; mix with hands to form soft dough.

2. Divide dough into 6 equal pieces and place, evenly spaced, on greased 15×10-inch jelly-roll pan. Spread dough evenly to edges of pan using hands; smooth top of dough with metal spatula or palms of hands. Mix remaining egg white and water in small cup; brush over top of dough. Lightly score dough into 2×1½-inch squares.

3. Bake 20 to 25 minutes or until lightly browned and firm when lightly touched with fingertip. Prepare Sugar Glaze. While still warm, cut along score lines into squares; drizzle or spread Sugar Glaze over squares. Let stand 15 minutes or until glaze is firm before removing from pan.

Sugar Glaze: Combine 1½ cups powdered sugar, 2 tablespoons milk and 1 teaspoon vanilla in small bowl. If glaze is too thick, add additional 1 tablespoon milk. Makes ¾ cup glaze.

Nutrients per serving: 1 cookie
Calories: 48, **Calories from Fat:** 18%, **Total Fat:** 1g,
Saturated Fat: <1g, **Cholesterol:** <1mg, **Sodium:** 35mg,
Carbohydrate: 9g, **Fiber:** <1g, **Protein:** 1g

Dietary Exchange: ½ Starch

Chocolate-Almond Meringue Puffs

Makes 15 servings

- 2 tablespoons granulated sugar
- 3 packets sugar substitute
- 1½ teaspoons unsweetened cocoa powder
- 2 egg whites, at room temperature
- ½ teaspoon vanilla
- ¼ teaspoon cream of tartar
- ¼ teaspoon almond extract
- ⅛ teaspoon salt
- 1½ ounces sliced almonds
- 3 tablespoons sugar-free seedless raspberry fruit spread

1. Preheat oven to 275°F. Combine granulated sugar, sugar substitute and cocoa in small bowl; set aside.

2. Place egg whites in small bowl; beat at high speed of electric mixer until foamy. Add vanilla, cream of tartar, almond extract and salt; beat until soft peaks form. Add sugar mixture, 1 tablespoon at a time, beating until stiff peaks form.

3. Line baking sheet with foil. Spoon 15 equal mounds of egg white mixture onto foil. Sprinkle with almonds.

4. Bake 1 hour. Turn oven off but do not open door. Leave puffs in oven 2 hours longer or until completely dry. Remove from oven; cool completely.

5. Stir fruit spread and spoon about ½ teaspoon onto each meringue just before serving.

Tip: Puffs are best if eaten the same day they're made. If necessary, store in airtight container, adding fruit topping at time of serving.

Nutrients per serving: 1 Puff with ½ teaspoon fruit spread
Calories: 36, **Calories from Fat:** 25%, **Total Fat:** 1g,
Saturated Fat: <1g, **Sodium:** 27mg, **Carbohydrate:** 5g, **Fiber:** <1g,
Protein: 1g

Dietary Exchange: ½ Starch

Tangy Lemon Squares

Makes 16 servings

- ¾ cup all-purpose flour
- ⅓ cup EQUAL® SPOONFUL*
- ⅛ teaspoon salt
- 6 tablespoons cold stick butter or margarine, cut into pieces
- 1 teaspoon grated lemon peel
- 1 teaspoon vanilla
- 2 eggs
- ¾ cup EQUAL® SPOONFUL**
- ½ cup lemon juice
- 4 tablespoons stick butter or margarine, melted
- 1 tablespoon grated lemon peel

*May substitute 8 packets EQUAL® sweetener.

**May substitute 18 packets EQUAL® sweetener.

• Combine flour, ⅓ cup EQUAL® Spoonful and salt in medium bowl. Cut in 6 tablespoons butter with pastry blender until mixture resembles coarse crumbs. Sprinkle with 1 teaspoon lemon peel and vanilla; mix with hands to form dough.

• Press dough evenly on bottom and ¼-inch up sides of 8-inch square baking pan. Bake in preheated 350°F oven 8 to 10 minutes. Cool on wire rack.

• Beat eggs and ¾ cup EQUAL® Spoonful; mix in lemon juice, 4 tablespoons melted butter and 1 tablespoon lemon peel. Pour mixture into baked pastry.

• Bake until lemon filling is set, about 15 minutes. Cool completely on wire rack.

Nutrients per serving: 1 square
Calories: 97, **Calories from Fat:** 74% **Total Fat:** 8g,
Saturated Fat: 4g, **Cholesterol:** 46mg, **Sodium:** 101mg,
Carbohydrate: 5g, **Protein:** 2g

Dietary Exchange: ½ Starch, 1½ Fat

Double Chocolate Brownies

Makes 16 servings

1 cup EQUAL® SPOONFUL*
¾ cup all-purpose flour
½ cup semi-sweet chocolate chips or mini chocolate chips
6 tablespoons unsweetened cocoa
1 teaspoon baking powder
¼ teaspoon salt
6 tablespoons stick butter or margarine, softened
½ cup unsweetened applesauce
2 eggs
1 teaspoon vanilla

May substitute 24 packets EQUAL® sweetener.

• Combine Equal®, flour, chocolate chips, cocoa, baking powder and salt. Beat butter, applesauce, eggs and vanilla until blended. Stir in combined flour mixture until blended.

• Spread batter in 8-inch square baking pan sprayed with nonstick cooking spray. Bake in preheated 350°F oven 18 to 20 minutes or until top springs back when gently touched. Cool completely on wire rack.

Nutrients per serving: 1 brownie (¹⁄₁₆ of total recipe)
Calories: 108, **Calories from Fat:** 58%, **Total Fat:** 7g,
Saturated Fat: 4g, **Cholesterol:** 38mg, **Sodium:** 119mg,
Carbohydrate: 10g, **Fiber:** 1g, **Protein:** 2g

Dietary Exchange: 1 Starch, 1 Fat

Peanut Butter Chocolate Bars

Makes 48 bars

1 cup EQUAL® SPOONFUL*
½ cup stick butter or margarine, softened
⅓ cup firmly packed brown sugar
½ cup 2% milk
½ cup creamy peanut butter
1 egg
1 teaspoon vanilla
1 cup all-purpose flour
¾ cup quick oats, uncooked
½ teaspoon baking soda
¼ teaspoon salt
¾ cup mini semi-sweet chocolate chips

May substitute 24 packets EQUAL® sweetener.

• Beat Equal®, butter and brown sugar until well combined. Stir in milk, peanut butter, egg and vanilla until blended. Gradually mix in combined flour, oats, baking soda and salt until blended. Stir in chocolate chips.

• Spread mixture evenly in 13×9-inch baking pan generously coated with nonstick cooking spray. Bake in preheated 350°F oven 20 to 22 minutes. Cool completely in pan on wire rack. Cut into squares; store in airtight container at room temperature.

Nutrients per serving: 1 bar
Calories: 68, **Calories from Fat:** 53%, **Total Fat:** 4g,
Saturated Fat: 2g, **Cholesterol:** 10mg, **Sodium:** 60mg,
Carbohydrate: 7g, **Fiber:** 1g, **Protein:** 1g

Dietary Exchange: ½ Starch, 1 Fat

Peanut Butter Chocolate Bars

Pumpkin Polka Dot Cookies

Makes about 4 dozen cookies

> 1¼ cups EQUAL® SPOONFUL*
> ½ cup (1 stick) butter or margarine, softened
> 3 tablespoons light molasses
> 1 cup canned pumpkin
> 1 egg
> 1½ teaspoons vanilla
> 1⅔ cups all-purpose flour
> 1 teaspoon baking powder
> 1¼ teaspoons ground cinnamon
> ½ teaspoon ground nutmeg
> ½ teaspoon ground ginger
> ½ teaspoon baking soda
> ¼ teaspoon salt
> 1 cup mini semi-sweet chocolate chips

May substitute 30 packets EQUAL® sweetener.

• Beat Equal®, butter and molasses until well combined. Mix in pumpkin, egg and vanilla until blended. Gradually stir in combined flour, baking powder, spices, baking soda and salt until well blended. Stir in chocolate chips.

• Drop by teaspoonfuls onto baking sheet sprayed with nonstick cooking spray. Bake in preheated 350°F oven 11 to 13 minutes. Remove from baking sheet and cool completely on wire rack. Store at room temperature in airtight container up to 1 week.

Nutrients per serving: 1 cookie
Calories: 63, **Calories from Fat:** 43%, **Total Fat:** 3g,
Saturated Fat: 2g, **Cholesterol:** 10mg, **Sodium:** 69mg,
Carbohydrate: 8g, **Fiber:** 1g, **Protein:** 1g

Dietary Exchange: ½ Starch, ½ Fat

Raspberry-Almond Bars

Makes 24 servings

- 2 **cups all-purpose flour**
- ½ **cup EQUAL® SPOONFUL***
- ⅛ **teaspoon salt**
- 8 **tablespoons cold margarine or butter, cut into pieces**
- 1 **large egg**
- 1 **tablespoon fat-free milk or water**
- 2 **teaspoons grated lemon peel**
- ⅔ **cup seedless raspberry spreadable fruit**
- 1 **teaspoon cornstarch**
- ½ **cup sliced toasted almonds, or walnut or pecan pieces**

*May substitute 12 packets EQUAL® sweetener.

- Combine flour, Equal® and salt in medium bowl; cut in margarine with pastry blender until mixture resembles coarse crumbs. Mix in egg, milk and lemon peel (mixture will be crumbly).

- Press mixture evenly in bottom of greased 11×7-inch baking dish. Bake in preheated 400°F oven until edges of crust are browned, about 15 minutes. Cool on wire rack.

- Mix spreadable fruit and cornstarch in small saucepan; heat to boiling. Boil until thickened, stirring constantly, 1 minute; cool until warm. Spread mixture evenly over cooled crust; sprinkle with almonds. Bake in preheated 400°F oven until spreadable fruit is thick and bubbly, about 15 minutes. Cool on wire rack; cut into bars.

Nutrients per serving: 1 bar
Calories: 116, **Calories from Fat:** 47%, **Total Fat:** 6g, **Cholesterol:** 9mg, **Sodium:** 59mg, **Carbohydrate:** 15g, **Protein:** 2g

Dietary Exchange: 1 Starch, 1 Fat

Peanut Butter & Banana Cookies

Makes 2 dozen cookies

- ¼ **cup (½ stick) butter**
- ½ **cup mashed ripe banana**
- ½ **cup no-sugar-added natural peanut butter**
- ¼ **cup thawed frozen unsweetened apple juice concentrate**
- 1 **egg**
- 1 **teaspoon vanilla**
- 1 **cup all-purpose flour**
- ½ **teaspoon baking soda**
- ¼ **teaspoon salt**
- ½ **cup chopped salted peanuts**
  Whole salted peanuts (optional)

Preheat oven to 375°F. Grease cookie sheets. Beat butter in large bowl with electric mixer until creamy. Add banana and peanut butter; beat until smooth. Blend in apple juice concentrate, egg and vanilla. Beat in flour, baking soda and salt. Stir in chopped peanuts. Drop rounded tablespoonfuls of dough 2 inches apart onto prepared cookie sheets; top each with one whole peanut, if desired. Bake 8 minutes or until set. Cool completely on wire racks. Store in tightly covered container.

Nutrients per serving: 1 cookie
Calories: 100, **Calories from Fat:** 53%, **Total Fat:** 6g, **Saturated Fat:** 2g, **Cholesterol:** 14mg, **Sodium:** 88mg, **Carbohydrate:** 9g, **Fiber:** 1g, **Protein:** 3g

Dietary Exchange: ½ Starch, 1½ Fat

Double Chocolate Biscotti

Makes 24 servings

- ¾ **cup all-purpose flour**
- 3 **tablespoons sugar substitute**
- 3 **tablespoons brown sugar**
- 2 **tablespoons unsweetened cocoa**
- 1 **teaspoon baking powder**
- ¼ **teaspoon salt**
- 2 **tablespoons butter**
- 1 **tablespoon chocolate syrup**
- 2 **egg whites, softly beaten**
- ½ **cup puffed wheat cereal**
- 4 **teaspoons sliced almonds**

1. Preheat oven to 350°F. Line baking sheet with parchment paper; set aside.

2. Mix flour, sugar substitute, brown sugar, cocoa, baking powder, salt and flour in medium bowl. Set aside.

3. Melt butter in small saucepan until golden brown. Remove from heat and pour into another bowl. Add chocolate syrup and egg whites. Stir butter mixture into dry ingredients to form stiff dough. Stir in cereal.

4. Turn dough out onto baking sheet and shape into a 12-inch log, 2 inches wide. Press almonds onto log. Bake 20 to 25 minutes or until firm.

5. Remove from oven and cool completely. Use sharp serrated knife to slice loaf into ½-inch thick diagonal slices. Place slices, cut-side down, on baking sheet. *Reduce oven temperature to 300°F.* Bake biscotti 10 minutes. Remove from oven and turn over biscotti slices to other side. Bake 10 minutes. Cool on wire rack.

Nutrients per serving: 1 biscotti
Calories: 38, **Calories from Fat:** 47%, **Total Fat:** 2g,
Saturated Fat: <1g, **Cholesterol:** 3mg, **Sodium:** 58mg,
Carbohydrate: 6g, **Fiber:** <1g, **Protein:** 1g

Dietary Exchange: ½ Starch

Cheery Cherry Brownies

Makes 12 servings

- ¾ **cup all-purpose flour**
- ½ **cup sugar substitute**
- ½ **cup unsweetened cocoa powder**
- ¼ **teaspoon baking soda**
- ½ **cup evaporated skimmed milk**
- ⅓ **cup butter, melted**
- ¼ **cup cholesterol-free egg substitute**
- ¼ **cup honey**
- 1 **teaspoon vanilla**
- ½ **(15½-ounce) can pitted tart red cherries, drained and halved**

1. Preheat oven to 350°F. Grease 11×7-inch baking pan; set aside.

2. Stir together flour, sugar substitute, cocoa and baking soda in large mixing bowl. Add milk, butter, egg substitute, honey and vanilla. Stir just until blended.

3. Pour into prepared pan. Sprinkle cherries over top of chocolate mixture. Bake 13 to 15 minutes or until toothpick inserted into center comes out clean. Cool completely in pan on wire rack. Cut into 12 equal-size brownies.

Nutrients per serving: 1 Brownie
Calories: 130, **Calories from Fat:** 42%, **Total Fat:** 6g,
Saturated Fat: 4g, **Cholesterol:** 28mg, **Sodium:** 110mg,
Carbohydrate: 18g, **Fiber:** 2g, **Protein:** 3g

Dietary Exchange: 1 Starch, 1 Fat

Cheery Cherry Brownie

cakes & cheesecakes

Chilled Cherry Cheesecake

Makes 9 servings

- 4 chocolate graham crackers, crushed
  (1 cup crumbs)
- 12 ounces Neufchâtel cheese
- 1 cup (8 ounces) vanilla-flavored fat-free yogurt
- ¼ cup sugar
- 1 teaspoon vanilla
- 1 envelope unflavored gelatin
- ¼ cup cold water
- 1 can (20 ounces) light cherry pie filling

1. Sprinkle cracker crumbs onto bottom of 8-inch square baking pan. Beat cheese, yogurt, sugar and vanilla in medium bowl with electric mixer at medium speed until smooth and creamy.

2. Sprinkle gelatin into water in small cup; let stand 2 minutes. Microwave at HIGH 40 seconds; stir and let stand 2 minutes or until gelatin is completely dissolved.

3. Gradually beat gelatin mixture into cheese mixture with electric mixer until well blended. Pour into prepared pan; refrigerate until firm. Spoon cherry filling onto cheesecake. Refrigerate until ready to serve.

Nutrients per serving: 1 serving (⅑ of total recipe)
Calories: 221, **Calories from Fat:** 41%, **Total Fat:** 10g,
Saturated Fat: 6g, **Cholesterol:** 29mg, **Sodium:** 226mg,
Carbohydrate: 29g, **Fiber:** 1g, **Protein:** 5g

Dietary Exchange: 2 Starch, 1½ Fat

Pear-Ginger Upside-Down Cake

Makes 8 servings

2 unpeeled Bosc or Anjou pears, cored and sliced into
¼-inch-thick pieces
3 tablespoons fresh lemon juice
1 to 2 tablespoons melted butter
1 to 2 tablespoons packed brown sugar
1 cup all-purpose flour
1 teaspoon baking powder
1 teaspoon ground cinnamon
¼ teaspoon baking soda
⅛ teaspoon salt
⅓ cup fat-free (skim) milk
3 tablespoons no-sugar-added apricot fruit spread
1 egg
1 tablespoon vegetable oil
1 tablespoon minced fresh ginger

1. Preheat oven to 375°F. Spray 10-inch deep-dish pie pan with nonstick cooking spray; set aside.

2. Toss pears in lemon juice; drain. Brush butter evenly onto bottom of prepared pan; sprinkle sugar over butter. Arrange pears in pan; bake 10 minutes.

3. Meanwhile, combine flour, baking powder, cinnamon, baking soda and salt in small bowl; set aside. Combine milk, apricot spread, egg, oil and ginger in medium bowl; mix well. Add flour mixture; stir until well mixed. (Batter will be very thick.) Carefully spread batter evenly over pears to edge of pan.

4. Bake 20 to 25 minutes or until light brown and toothpick inserted into center comes out clean.

5. Remove pan to wire rack; cool 5 minutes. Use knife to loosen cake from side of pan. Place 10-inch plate over top of pan; quickly turn over to transfer cake to plate. Place any pears left in pan on top of cake. Serve warm.

Nutrients per serving: 1 slice cake (⅛ of total recipe)
Calories: 139, **Calories from Fat:** 26%, **Total Fat:** 4g,
Saturated Fat: 1g, **Cholesterol:** 31mg, **Sodium:** 174mg,
Carbohydrate: 23g, **Fiber:** 2g, **Protein:** 3g

Dietary Exchange: 1½ Starch, ½ Fat

Pear-Ginger Upside-Down Cake

Fresh Apple-Pecan Coffee Cake

Makes 16 servings

> 1 **package (16.9-ounce) cinnamon-swirl quick-bread and coffeecake mix**
> ¾ **cup water**
> 4 **egg whites** *or* ½ **cup cholesterol-free egg substitute**
> 1 **teaspoon vanilla or vanilla, butter and nut flavoring**
> 1 **cup finely chopped apples***

*Granny Smith apples are recommended for this recipe.

1. Preheat oven to 350°F. Spray 13×9-inch baking pan with nonstick cooking spray; set aside.

2. Combine quick-bread mix, water, egg whites and vanilla in medium bowl; beat 50 strokes or until well blended. Spoon batter into prepared baking pan. Smooth evenly with back of spoon.

3. Sprinkle apples evenly over batter. Sprinkle cinnamon swirl mix evenly over all. Bake 22 minutes or until toothpick inserted into center comes out clean.

4. Remove cake to wire rack; cool 15 minutes. Cut into 16 pieces. Serve warm or at room temperature.

Prep Time: 10 minutes
Bake Time: 22 minutes
Cool Time: 15 minutes

Note: Flavors are at their peak when this coffeecake is served warm. To reheat, place in a microwave and cook on HIGH 10 to 15 seconds or until heated.

Nutrients per serving: 1 piece coffee cake (1/16 of total recipe)
Calories: 140, **Calories from Fat:** 26%, **Total Fat:** 4g,
Saturated Fat: 1g, **Sodium:** 131mg, **Carbohydrate:** 24g,
Fiber: <1g, **Protein:** 2g

Dietary Exchange: 1 Starch, ½ Fruit, ½ Fat

cakes & cheesecakes

Chocolate Cherry Cups

Makes 12 servings

- ⅓ cup all-purpose flour
- ⅓ cup sugar
- ¼ cup ground baking chocolate
- ¼ cup cocoa powder
- ¼ teaspoon baking powder
- ¼ teaspoon salt
- 3 egg whites
- 1 container (6 ounces) vanilla-flavored fat-free yogurt
- ½ teaspoon almond extract
- Nonstick cooking spray
- 36 frozen drained pitted sour cherries, without sugar, thawed

1. Preheat oven to 350°F. Line 12 standard (2½-inch) muffin pan cups with foil baking cups. Place flour, sugar, ground chocolate, cocoa powder, baking powder and salt in medium bowl. Whisk until combined.

2. Beat egg whites in medium bowl with electric mixer at high speed until soft peaks form. Add yogurt to dry mixture. Stir well, scraping sides of bowl. Fold in beaten egg whites and almond extract.

3. Fill prepared muffin cups two-thirds full. Place 3 cherries into each cup, pressing lightly into batter.

4. Bake 20 to 25 minutes until tops are puffy and edges are set. Centers will be moist.

Nutrients per serving: 1 Cherry Cup
Calories: 63, **Calories from Fat:** 16%, **Total Fat:** <2g,
Saturated Fat: <1g, **Cholesterol:** <1mg, **Sodium:** 83mg,
Carbohydrate: 12g, **Fiber:** 1g, **Protein:** 3g

Dietary Exchange: 1 Starch, ½ Fruit

cakes & cheesecakes

Apricot Walnut Swirl Coffeecake

Makes 12 servings

WALNUT FILLING
- ½ cup sugar-free apricot preserves or apricot spreadable fruit
- ¾ cup EQUAL® SPOONFUL*
- 4 teaspoons ground cinnamon
- ½ cup chopped walnuts

COFFEECAKE
- 2⅓ cups reduced-fat baking mix (Bisquick®)
- ½ cup EQUAL® SPOONFUL**
- ⅔ cup fat-free milk
- ⅓ cup fat-free sour cream
- 1 egg
- 2 tablespoons stick butter or margarine, melted
- ⅓ cup sugar-free apricot preserves or apricot spreadable fruit

May substitute 18 packets EQUAL® sweetener.

**May substitute 12 packets EQUAL® sweetener.*

• For Walnut Filling, mix ½ cup apricot preserves, ¾ cup Equal® Spoonful, cinnamon and walnuts in small bowl.

• For Coffeecake, combine baking mix and ½ cup Equal® Spoonful; mix in milk, sour cream, egg and butter. Spread ⅓ of batter in greased and floured 6-cup bundt pan; spoon half of Walnut Filling over batter. Repeat layers, ending with batter.

• Bake in preheated 375°F oven about 25 minutes or until coffeecake is browned on top and toothpick inserted into center comes out clean. Cool in pan 5 minutes; invert onto wire rack and cool 5 to 10 minutes.

• Spoon ⅓ cup apricot preserves over top of coffeecake; serve warm.

Nutrients per serving: 1 slice coffeecake (¹⁄₁₂ of total recipe)
Calories: 189, **Calories from Fat:** 33%, **Total Fat:** 7g,
Saturated Fat: 1g, **Cholesterol:** 18mg, **Sodium:** 332mg,
Carbohydrate: 28g, **Fiber:** 1g, **Protein:** 4g

Dietary Exchange: 2 Starch, 1 Fat

Java-Spiked Walnut Coffee Cake

Makes 9 servings

    2 tablespoons sugar-free fat-free mocha instant
      coffee mix
 ¼ teaspoon ground cinnamon
1½ cups all-purpose flour
 ¼ cup granular sugar substitute*
 ¼ cup granulated sugar
  1 teaspoon baking powder
 ½ teaspoon baking soda
 ⅛ teaspoon salt
  1 container (6 ounces) plain fat-free yogurt
 ¼ cup cholesterol-free egg substitute
  2 tablespoons butter, melted
  1 teaspoon vanilla
 ¼ cup finely chopped walnuts

This recipe was tested with sucralose-based sugar substitute.

1. Preheat oven to 350°F. Spray 8×8×2-inch baking pan with nonstick cooking spray; set aside.

2. Combine coffee mix and cinnamon in small bowl; set aside.

3. Combine flour, sugar substitute, sugar, baking powder, baking soda and salt in large bowl. Combine yogurt, egg substitute, butter and vanilla in small bowl; add to flour mixture. Stir just until moistened.

4. Spread batter into prepared pan. Sprinkle with reserved coffee mixture. Sprinkle with walnuts. Bake 30 to 35 minutes or until toothpick inserted into center comes out clean. Serve warm. Cut into 9 pieces.

Prep Time: 30 minutes
Bake Time: 30 minutes

Nutrients per serving: 1 piece coffee cake
Calories: 166, **Calories from Fat:** 28%, **Total Fat:** 5g,
Saturated Fat: 2g, **Cholesterol:** 8mg, **Sodium:** 212mg,
Carbohydrate: 25g, **Fiber:** 1g, **Protein:** 4g

Dietary Exchange: 2 Starch, 1 Fat

Java-Spiked Walnut Coffee Cake

Chocolate Orange Cake Roll

Makes 10 servings

⅓ **cup all-purpose flour**
¼ **cup plus 1 tablespoon unsweetened cocoa powder,
   divided**
¼ **teaspoon baking soda**
4 **eggs, separated**
½ **teaspoon vanilla**
¼ **cup sugar substitute***
½ **cup plus 2 tablespoons sugar, divided**
½ **cup orange fruit spread**

*This recipe was tested with sucralose-based sugar substitute.

1. Preheat oven to 375°F. Spray 15×10×1-inch jelly-roll pan with nonstick cooking spray. Dust with flour. Set aside.

2. Combine flour, ¼ cup cocoa and baking soda in small bowl; set aside.

3. Beat 4 egg yolks and vanilla in large bowl with electric mixer at high speed 5 to 6 minutes or until thick and light colored. Gradually add sugar substitute and 2 tablespoons granulated sugar, beating well after each addition.

4. Beat 4 egg whites in another large bowl with electric mixer at high speed until soft peaks form. Gradually add remaining ½ cup granulated sugar; beat until stiff peaks form.

5. Gently fold egg yolk mixture into egg white mixture. Sift flour mixture over egg mixture. Gently fold flour mixture into egg mixture just until blended. Spread evenly into prepared pan. Bake 12 to 15 minutes or until top springs back when lightly touched.

6. Meanwhile, sprinkle remaining 1 tablespoon cocoa onto one side of clean towel. Use narrow spatula to loosen edges of cake from pan. Invert pan onto prepared towel. Roll up towel and cake, starting from short side. Cool on wire rack. Unroll cake. Remove towel. Spread cake with orange spread. Roll up cake. Cut into 10 slices.

Nutrients per serving: 1 slice cake roll (¹⁄₁₀ of total recipe)
Calories: 136, **Calories from Fat:** 13%, **Total Fat:** 2g,
Saturated Fat: 1g, **Cholesterol:** 85mg, **Sodium:** 60mg,
Carbohydrate: 25g, **Fiber:** 1g, **Protein:** 3g

Dietary Exchange: 1½ Starch, ½ Fat

Chocolate Orange Cake Roll

56

cakes & cheesecakes

Pumpkin-Fig Cheesecake

Makes 16 slices

- **12** nonfat fig bar cookies
- **2** packages (8 ounces each) fat-free cream cheese, softened
- **1** package (8 ounces) reduced-fat cream cheese, softened
- **1** can (15 ounces) pumpkin
- **1** cup SPLENDA® No Calorie Sweetener, Granular
- **1** cup cholesterol-free egg substitute
- **½** cup nonfat evaporated milk
- **1** tablespoon vanilla extract
- **2** teaspoons pumpkin pie spice mix
- **¼** teaspoon salt
- **½** cup chopped dried figs
- **2** tablespoons walnut pieces

1. Preheat oven to 325°F. Lightly coat 8- or 9-inch springform baking pan with nonstick cooking spray.

2. Break up cookies with fingers, then chop by hand with knife or process in food processor until crumbly. Lightly press cookie crumbs onto bottom and side of pan. Bake 15 minutes; cool slightly while preparing filling.

3. In large bowl, beat cream cheese with mixer at high speed until smooth. Add pumpkin, SPLENDA®, egg substitute, milk, vanilla, spice mix and salt. Beat until smooth. Spread filling evenly over crust.

4. Place springform pan on baking sheet. Bake 1 hour and 15 minutes or until top begins to crack and center moves very little when pan is jiggled. Cool on wire rack to room temperature; refrigerate 4 to 6 hours or overnight before serving.

5. Just before serving, arrange figs and nuts around top edge of cheesecake.

Nutrients per serving: 1 slice cheesecake (¹⁄₁₆ of total recipe)
Calories: 157, **Calories from Fat:** 17%, **Total Fat:** 3g,
Saturated Fat: 2g, **Cholesterol:** 9mg, **Sodium:** 310mg,
Carbohydrate: 22g, **Fiber:** 2g, **Protein:** 9g

Dietary Exchange: 1½ Starch, 1 Meat

Pumpkin-Fig Cheesecake

Chocolate-Berry Cheesecake

Makes 16 servings

- 1 cup chocolate wafer crumbs
- 1 container (12 ounces) fat-free cream cheese
- 1 package (8 ounces) reduced-fat cream cheese
- ⅔ cup sugar
- ½ cup cholesterol-free egg substitute
- 3 tablespoons fat-free (skim) milk
- 1¼ teaspoons vanilla
- 1 cup mini semisweet chocolate chips
- 2 tablespoons raspberry all-fruit spread
- 2 tablespoons water
- 2½ cups fresh strawberries, hulled and halved

1. Preheat oven to 350°F. Spray bottom of 9-inch springform pan with nonstick cooking spray.

2. Press chocolate wafer crumbs firmly onto bottom of prepared pan. Bake 10 minutes. Remove from oven; cool. *Reduce oven temperature to 325°F.*

3. Combine cheeses in large bowl with electric mixer. Beat at medium speed until well blended. Beat in sugar until well blended. Beat in egg substitute, milk and vanilla until well blended. Stir in mini chips with spoon. Pour batter into pan.

4. Bake 40 minutes or until center is set. Remove from oven; cool 10 minutes in pan on wire rack. Carefully loosen cheesecake from edge of pan. Cool completely.

5. Remove side of pan from cake. Blend fruit spread and water in medium bowl until smooth. Add strawberries; toss to coat. Arrange strawberries on top of cake. Refrigerate 1 hour before serving. Garnish with fresh mint, if desired.

Nutrients per serving: 1 slice (¹⁄₁₆ of total recipe)

Calories: 197, **Calories from Fat:** 32%, **Total Fat:** 7g, **Saturated Fat:** 2g, **Cholesterol:** 7mg, **Sodium:** 290mg, **Carbohydrate:** 29g, **Fiber:** <1g, **Protein:** 7g

Dietary Exchange: 1 Starch, 1 Fruit, ½ Meat, 1 Fat

pies & tarts

Banana Pistachio Pie

Makes 8 servings

- ¾ cup cinnamon graham cracker crumbs
- 2 tablespoons reduced-fat margarine, melted
- 2 packages (4-serving size each) fat-free sugar-free instant pistachio pudding and pie filling mix
- 2½ cups fat-free (skim) milk
- 1 large ripe banana, sliced
- ¼ teaspoon ground cinnamon
- 1 cup thawed reduced-fat nondairy whipped topping
- Additional thawed frozen reduced-fat whipped topping (optional)

1. Combine graham cracker crumbs and margarine in small bowl; stir with fork until crumbly. Press crumb mixture onto bottom of 9-inch pie plate.

2. Prepare pudding mix according to package directions for pie filling, using 2½ cups milk. Gently stir in banana and cinnamon; fold in 1 cup whipped topping. Pour into prepared crust. Refrigerate at least 1 hour. Top with additional whipped topping before serving, if desired.

Nutrients per serving: 1 slice pie (⅛ of total recipe) without additional whipped topping
Calories: 143, **Calories from Fat:** 25%, **Total Fat:** 4g, **Saturated Fat:** 1g, **Cholesterol:** 2mg, **Sodium:** 450mg, **Carbohydrate:** 22g, **Fiber:** 1g, **Protein:** 3g

Dietary Exchange: 1½ Starch, 1 Fat

Raspberry Cheese Tarts

Makes 10 servings

CRUST

1¼ cups graham cracker crumbs

5 tablespoons light margarine (50% less fat and calories)

¼ cup SPLENDA® No Calorie Sweetener, Granular

FILLING

4 ounces reduced-fat cream cheese

½ cup plain nonfat yogurt

1 cup SPLENDA® No Calorie Sweetener, Granular

½ cup egg substitute

1 cup frozen raspberries

CRUST

1. Preheat oven to 350°F. In medium bowl, mix together graham cracker crumbs, margarine, and ¼ cup SPLENDA®. Press about 1 tablespoon of crust mixture into 10 muffin pan cups lined with paper liners. Set aside.

FILLING

2. In small bowl, beat cream cheese with electric mixer on low speed until soft, about 30 seconds. Add yogurt and beat on low speed until smooth, approximately 1 minute. Stir in SPLENDA® and egg substitute until well blended.

3. Place 1½ tablespoons raspberries (4 to 5) into each muffin cup. Divide filling evenly among muffin cups. Bake for 20 minutes or until firm.

4. Refrigerate for 2 hours before serving. Garnish as desired.

Preparation Time: 25 minutes
Baking Time: 20 minutes
Chilling Time: 2 hours

Nutrients per serving: 1 tart or 2.6 ounces (82 g)
Calories: 140, **Calories from Fat:** 39%, **Total Fat:** 6g,
Saturated Fat: 2g, **Cholesterol:** 6mg, **Sodium:** 255mg,
Carbohydrate: 15g, **Fiber:** 1g, **Protein:** 5g

Dietary Exchange: 1 Starch, 1 Fat

Raspberry Cheese Tarts

No-Bake Coconut Cream Pie

Makes 12 servings

> 2 tablespoons water
> 1 envelope plain gelatin
> 1 can (14½ ounces) light coconut milk
> 1 package (8 ounces) fat-free cream cheese
> 9 packets sugar substitute, divided
> 2 teaspoons vanilla
> 1 teaspoon coconut extract
> 1 low-fat graham cracker pie crust
> ¼ cup unsweetened grated coconut

1. Place water in small microwave-safe bowl. Sprinkle gelatin over water and let stand 1 minute. Heat bowl in microwave on HIGH 20 seconds or until gelatin is completely dissolved.

2. In blender, combine coconut milk, cream cheese, 8 packets sugar substitute, vanilla, coconut extract and gelatin mixture. Cover tightly and blend until smooth. Pour mixture into prepared crust; cover and chill until firm, about 4 hours.

3. Before serving, toast coconut in nonstick skillet over low heat until golden brown. When cool, toss with remaining sugar substitute and sprinkle over pie.

Nutrients per serving: 1 slice pie (¹⁄₁₂ of total recipe)
Calories: 118, **Calories from Fat:** 38%, **Total Fat:** 5g,
Saturated Fat: 3g, **Cholesterol:** 2mg, **Sodium:** 175mg,
Carbohydrate: 13g, **Fiber:** <1g, **Protein:** 4g

Dietary Exchange: 1 Starch, 1 Fat

No-Bake Coconut Cream Pie

Fresh Strawberry Cream Pie

Makes 8 servings

> 1 quart fresh medium strawberries
> 1 tablespoon EQUAL® SPOONFUL*
>   Pastry for single-crust 9-inch pie, baked
> 1 package (8 ounces) reduced-fat cream cheese, softened
> ⅓ cup vanilla-flavored light nonfat yogurt
> ¼ cup EQUAL® SPOONFUL**
> 1 tablespoon lemon juice

May substitute 1½ packets EQUAL® sweetener.

**May substitute 6 packets EQUAL® sweetener.*

• Remove stems from several strawberries and slice to make 1 cup. Toss with 1 tablespoon Equal® Spoonful. Spread on bottom of baked pie shell.

• Beat cream cheese, yogurt, ¼ cup Equal® Spoonful and 1 tablespoon lemon juice until smooth and fluffy. Spread over sliced strawberries in pie shell. Remove stems from all but 1 large strawberry. Cut berries lengthwise in half. Place, cut side down, over cream cheese mixture, around outer edge of pie crust, with pointed end of berries facing center of pie. Make several thin slits in last whole berry, starting near top and going to pointed end. Press gently with fingers to form "fan." Place on center of pie.

• Refrigerate pie at least 4 hours before serving.

Nutrients per serving: 1 slice pie (⅛ of total recipe)
Calories: 185, **Calories from Fat:** 44%, **Total Fat:** 9g,
Saturated Fat: 6g, **Cholesterol:** 13mg, **Sodium:** 144mg,
Carbohydrate: 13g, **Fiber:** 1g, **Protein:** 4g

Dietary Exchange: ½ Starch, ½ Fruit, 2½ Fat

Fresh Strawberry Cream Pie

Triple Berry Tart

Makes 8 servings

> 1 unbaked (9-inch) pie crust
> ¼ cup raspberry all-fruit spread
> 1½ cups fat-free whipped topping
> 3 ounces reduced-fat cream cheese, softened
> 1½ cups strawberry halves or quarters, stems removed
> ½ cup fresh raspberries
> ½ cup fresh or frozen blueberries, thawed
> 1 tablespoon powdered sugar

1. Preheat oven to 450°F.

2. Unroll pie crust on large nonstick baking sheet; prick with fork. Bake 8 minutes or until light brown. Remove to wire rack; cool completely.

3. Place fruit spread in small microwavable bowl; microwave at HIGH 15 seconds or until slightly melted. Remove from microwave. Spread evenly over pie crust, leaving ½-inch edge.

4. Beat whipped topping with cream cheese in medium bowl with electric mixer on medium speed until well blended and smooth. Spoon tablespoonfuls whipped topping mixture evenly over fruit spread. Using back of spoon, smooth whipped topping layer.

5. Arrange berries in decorative fashion over top. Sprinkle with powdered sugar.

Nutrients per serving: 1 wedge (⅛ of total recipe)
Calories: 171, **Calories from Fat:** 37%, **Total Fat:** 7g,
Saturated Fat: 2g, **Cholesterol:** 6mg, **Sodium:** 143mg,
Carbohydrate: 24g, **Fiber:** 1g, **Protein:** 2g

Dietary Exchange: 1 Starch, ½ Fruit, 1½ Fat

Triple Berry Tart

Peppermint Ice Cream Pie

Makes 12 servings

- 4 cups no-sugar-added vanilla ice cream
- 6 sugar-free peppermint candies
- 1 reduced-fat graham cracker pie crust
- ¼ cup sugar-free chocolate syrup

1. Scoop ice cream into medium bowl; let stand at room temperature 5 minutes or until softened, stirring occasionally.

2. Place candies in heavy-duty plastic food storage bag; coarsely crush with rolling pin or meat mallet. Stir candy into ice cream; spread evenly into pie crust.

3. Cover pie; freeze at least 4 hours or overnight. Using sharp knife that has been dipped in warm water, cut pie into 12 slices. Transfer to serving plates; drizzle with chocolate. Garnish, if desired.

Nutrients per serving: 1 slice pie (1/12 of total recipe)
Calories: 147, **Calories from Fat:** 24%, **Total Fat:** 4g,
Saturated Fat: 1g, **Sodium:** 134mg, **Carbohydrate:** 26g,
Fiber: 1g, **Protein:** 3g

Dietary Exchange: 2 Starch, ½ Fat

Peppermint Ice Cream Pie

pies & tarts

Lattice-Topped Deep Dish Cherry Pie

Makes 9 servings

> **2** cans (14½ ounces each) pitted red tart cherries in water
> **½** cup sugar substitute*
> **3** tablespoons quick-cooking tapioca
> **¼** teaspoon almond extract
> **¾** cup all-purpose flour
> **¼** teaspoon salt
> **3** tablespoons shortening
> **2 to 3** tablespoons cold water

This recipe was tested with sucralose-based sugar substitute.

1. Preheat oven to 375°F. Drain 1 can of cherries. Combine drained cherries, can of cherries with juice, sugar substitute, tapioca and almond extract in large bowl. Let stand while preparing crust.

2. Combine flour and salt in small bowl. Cut in shortening until mixture resembles fine crumbs. Add water, 1 tablespoon at a time, stirring just until dough is moistened. Form dough into ball. Roll dough into 9×8-inch rectangle on lightly floured surface. Cut into 9 (8×1-inch) strips.

3. Spoon cherry mixture into 13×9-inch baking dish. Place 4 pastry strips horizontally across pan or weave as shown in photo. Weave remaining 5 pastry strips vertically across horizontal strips. Pinch strips at ends to seal. Bake 40 to 50 minutes or until fruit is bubbly and pastry is light brown. Remove to wire rack; cool slightly. To serve, spoon into bowls.

Prep Time: 15 minutes
Bake Time: 40 to 50 minutes

Nutrients per serving: ⅔ cup pie
Calories: 126, **Calories from Fat:** 29%, **Total Fat:** 4g,
Saturated Fat: 1g, **Sodium:** 72mg, **Carbohydrate:** 21g,
Fiber: 1g, **Protein:** 2g

Dietary Exchange: ½ Starch, 1 Fruit, 1 Fat

Lattice-Topped Deep Dish Cherry Pie

Blueberry-Pear Tart

Makes 8 servings

> 1 refrigerated pie crust
> 1 medium fully ripened pear, peeled, cored and thinly sliced
> 8 ounces fresh or thawed frozen blueberries or blackberries
> ⅓ cup no-sugar-added raspberry fruit spread
> ½ teaspoon grated fresh ginger

1. Preheat oven to 450°F.

2. Spray 9-inch tart pan with nonstick cooking spray. Place dough in pan; press against side of pan to form ½-inch edge. Prick dough with fork. Bake 12 minutes. Remove pan to wire rack; cool completely.

3. Arrange pears on bottom of cooled crust; top with blueberries.

4. Place fruit spread in small microwavable bowl. Cover with plastic wrap; microwave at HIGH 15 seconds; stir. If necessary, microwave additional 10 to 15 seconds or until spread is melted; stir. Add ginger; stir until blended. Let stand 30 seconds to thicken slightly. Pour mixture over fruit in crust. Refrigerate 2 hours. (Do not cover.) Cut into 8 slices before serving.

Prep Time: 10 minutes
Bake Time: 12 minutes
Chill Time: 2 hours

Nutrients per serving: 1 slice tart (⅛ of total recipe)
Calories: 179, **Calories from Fat:** 36%, **Total Fat:** 7g,
Saturated Fat: 3g, **Cholesterol:** 5mg, **Sodium:** 101mg,
Carbohydrate: 28g, **Fiber:** 2g, **Protein:** 1g

Dietary Exchange: 1 Starch, 1 Fruit, 1 Fat

Blueberry-Pear Tart

Lemon Cream Peach and Blueberry Pie

Makes 8 servings

- 2 cups low-fat (1%) milk
- ¼ cup cholesterol-free egg substitute
- 3 tablespoons cornstarch
- ⅛ teaspoon salt
- 7 packets sugar substitute*
- 1 teaspoon grated lemon peel
- 3 tablespoons lemon juice
- 1 teaspoon vanilla
- 1 (6-ounce) prepared graham cracker crust
- 1 cup sliced fresh or thawed frozen peaches, cubed
- ¾ cup fresh or frozen blueberries, thawed, rinsed and drained

*This recipe was tested with sucralose-based sugar substitute.

1. Combine milk, egg substitute, cornstarch and salt in medium saucepan; whisk until cornstarch is dissolved. Cook over medium heat, stirring constantly, about 5 minutes or until mixture comes to a boil and thickens. Stir in sugar substitute, lemon peel, lemon juice and vanilla. Transfer mixture to medium bowl.

2. Place sheet of plastic wrap on top of filling to prevent skin from forming. Let mixture cool to room temperature. Spoon into crust. Decoratively top with peaches and blueberries. Chill completely before slicing into 8 wedges to serve.

Prep Time: 15 minutes plus chilling time
Cook Time: 5 minutes

Hint: Substitute any of your favorite in-season fruits for the peaches and blueberries.

Nutrients per serving: 1 slice pie
Calories: 168, **Calories from Fat:** 32%, **Total Fat:** 6g,
Saturated Fat: 2g, **Cholesterol:** 3mg, **Sodium:** 200mg,
Carbohydrate: 25g, **Fiber:** 1g, **Protein:** 4g

Dietary Exchange: 1 Starch, ½ Fruit, ½ Milk, ½ Fat

no-bake **desserts**

Peach Tapioca

Makes 4 servings

- 2 **cups reduced-fat (2%) milk**
- 3 **tablespoons quick-cooking tapioca**
- 1 **egg, lightly beaten**
- 1½ **cups peeled, coarsely chopped peaches***
- 3 **tablespoons no-sugar-added apricot spread**
- 1 **teaspoon vanilla**

*If fresh peaches are not in season, use frozen peaches and add 1 to 2 packets sugar substitute or equivalent of 4 teaspoons sugar to milk mixture.

1. Combine milk, tapioca and egg in 1½-quart saucepan; let stand 5 minutes. Stir in peaches and apricot spread.

2. Cook and stir over medium heat until mixture comes to a rolling boil; cook 1 minute more. Remove from heat and stir in vanilla.

3. Cool slightly; stir. Place plastic wrap directly on surface of pudding; chill. Garnish as desired.

Nutrients per serving: ¼ of total recipe
Calories: 155, **Calories from Fat:** 23%, **Total Fat:** 4g,
Saturated Fat: 2g, **Cholesterol:** 62mg, **Sodium:** 92mg,
Carbohydrate: 25g, **Fiber:** 1g, **Protein:** 6g

Dietary Exchange: 1½ Fruit, ½ Milk, ½ Fat

Peach Tapioca

Blackberry Sorbet

Makes 2 servings

> 1 **(8-fluid-ounce) can chilled Vanilla GLUCERNA®
>   Shake**
> 1 **cup frozen whole blackberries, unsweetened**
> ½ **teaspoon cinnamon**
> ¼ **teaspoon nutmeg**
>   **Sugar substitute to taste**

1. Combine all ingredients in blender. Blend until thick.

2. Serve immediately or freeze 10 to 15 minutes.

Nutrients per serving: ¾ cup sorbet
Calories: 161, **Calories from Fat:** 34%, **Total Fat:** 6g,
Saturated Fat: 1g, **Cholesterol:** 1mg, **Sodium:** 106mg,
Carbohydrate: 23g, **Fiber:** 5g, **Protein:** 6g

Dietary Exchange: 1 Starch, 1 Fruit, 1 Fat

Blackberry Sorbet

no-bake **desserts**

Cocoa-Cherry Chill
Makes 8 servings

> 1 can (14½ ounces) tart cherries packed in water, undrained
> 1½ cups frozen pitted unsweetened dark Bing cherries
> 1 cup fat-free half-and-half
> ½ cup reduced-calorie chocolate syrup
> 1 teaspoon vanilla
> Mint sprigs for garnish (optional)
> Dark cherries for garnish (optional)

1. Place tart cherries with liquid, frozen Bing cherries, half-and-half and chocolate syrup in blender. Cover and process on HIGH until very smooth.

2. Add vanilla; blend until smooth, stopping to scrape down sides of blender as needed. Freeze cherry mixture in ice cream maker, according to manufacturer's instructions.

3. Garnish each serving with a mint sprig and cherry, if desired. For best flavor, let stand 15 minutes at room temperature before serving.

Nutrients per serving: ½ cup dessert
Calories: 62, **Calories from Fat:** 2%, **Total Fat:** <1g,
Saturated Fat: <1g, **Cholesterol:** 4mg, **Sodium:** 41mg,
Carbohydrate: 14g, **Fiber:** 1g, **Protein:** 2g

Dietary Exchange: 1 Fruit

Individual No-Bake Cheesecake Fruit Cups

Makes 4 servings

> 1 **cup quartered strawberries**
> 1 **cup diced peaches**
> 3 **tablespoons sugar substitute,* divided**
> ¼ **teaspoon ground ginger**
> 5 **ounces reduced-fat cream cheese, softened**
> 3 **tablespoons fat-free sour cream**
> 2 **tablespoons fat-free (skim) milk**
> 1 **teaspoon vanilla**
> ¼ **cup graham cracker crumbs****

*This recipe was tested with sucralose-based sugar substitute.

**Or, crush 2¼ whole graham crackers.

1. Combine strawberries, peaches, 1 tablespoon sugar substitute and ginger in medium bowl. Toss gently to blend. Set aside.

2. Beat cream cheese, sour cream, milk, vanilla and remaining 2 tablespoons sugar substitute in small bowl with electric mixer at medium speed until smooth.

3. Place about 3 tablespoons cream cheese mixture in four (4-ounce) custard cups. Sprinkle 1 tablespoon cracker crumbs evenly into each cup. Top with ½ cup berry mixture. Cover and refrigerate at least 1 hour.

Nutrients per serving: 1 ramekin (2 tablespoons cream cheese mixture, 2 tablespoons cracker crumbs and ½ cup fruit)
Calories: 115, **Calories from Fat:** 30%, **Total Fat:** 4g, **Saturated Fat:** <1g, **Cholesterol:** 12mg, **Sodium:** 162mg, **Carbohydrate:** 17g, **Fiber:** 2g, **Protein:** 4g

Dietary Exchange: ½ Starch, ½ Fruit, 1 Fat

Tempting Chocolate Mousse

Makes 6 servings

   1 **envelope unflavored gelatin**
2½ **cups nonfat milk**
   ¼ **cup HERSHEY'®S Cocoa or HERSHEY'®S SPECIAL DARK® Cocoa**
   1 **tablespoon cornstarch**
   1 **egg yolk**
   1 **teaspoon vanilla extract**
      Granulated sugar substitute to equal 8 teaspoons sugar
   1 **cup prepared sucrose-free whipped topping***

*Combine 1 envelope (1 ounce) sucrose-free dry whipped topping mix with ½ cup very cold water according to package directions. (This makes about 2 cups topping; use 1 cup topping for mousse. Reserve remainder for garnish, if desired.)

1. Sprinkle gelatin over milk in medium saucepan; let stand 5 minutes to soften. Stir in cocoa, cornstarch and egg yolk; cook over medium heat, stirring constantly with whisk, until mixture comes to a boil. Reduce heat to low; cook, stirring constantly, until mixture thickens slightly, about 1 minute.

2. Remove from heat; cool to lukewarm. Stir in vanilla and sugar substitute. Pour mixture into medium bowl. Refrigerate, stirring occasionally, until thickened, about 45 minutes.

3. Fold 1 cup prepared whipped topping into chocolate mixture. Spoon into 6 individual dessert dishes. Cover; refrigerate until firm. Garnish with remaining whipped topping, if desired.

Nutrients per serving: 1 dessert dish
Calories: 90, **Calories from Fat:** 30%, **Total Fat:** 3g,
Cholesterol: 35mg, **Sodium:** 55mg, **Carbohydrate:** 11g,
Protein: 9g

Dietary Exchange: ½ Starch, ½ Milk, ½ Lean Meat

Dreamy Orange Cheesecake Dip

Makes 12 servings

> 1 **package (8 ounces) reduced-fat cream cheese, softened**
> ½ **cup orange marmalade**
> ½ **teaspoon vanilla**
> **Grated orange peel (optional)**
> **Mint leaves (optional)**
> 2 **cups whole strawberries**
> 2 **cups cantaloupe chunks**
> 2 **cups apple slices**

1. Combine cream cheese, marmalade and vanilla in small bowl; mix well. Garnish with orange peel and mint leaves, if desired.

2. Serve with fruit dippers.

Note: Dip can be prepared ahead of time. Store, covered, in refrigerator for up to 2 days.

Nutrients per serving: 2 tablespoons dip with ½ cup fruit (without garnish)
Calories: 102, **Calories from Fat:** 35%, **Total Fat:** 4g, **Saturated Fat:** 2g, **Cholesterol:** 7mg, **Sodium:** 111mg, **Carbohydrate:** 18g, **Fiber:** 2g, **Protein:** 3g

Dietary Exchange: 1 Fruit, ½ Meat, ½ Fat

Dreamy Orange Cheesecake Dip

Ricotta Cheese and Blueberry Parfait

Makes 4 servings

> 1 **cup whole milk ricotta cheese**
> 1 **tablespoon powdered sugar**
> **Grated peel of 1 lemon**
> 1½ **cups fresh blueberries**

1. Combine ricotta cheese, sugar and lemon peel in medium bowl; stir well.

2. Place 3 tablespoons blueberries in each of 4 parfait glasses. Add ¼ cup ricotta cheese mixture; top with another 3 tablespoons blueberries. Garnish as desired.

Variation: If your carb count can stand it, sprinkle top with some chopped pecans or slivered almonds.

Nutrients per serving: ⅔ cup parfait
Calories: 145, **Calories from Fat:** 49%, **Total Fat:** 8g,
Saturated Fat: 5g, **Cholesterol:** 31mg, **Sodium:** 55mg,
Carbohydrate: 12g, **Fiber:** 2g, **Protein:** 7g

Dietary Exchange: 1 Fruit, 1 Milk, 1 Meat, 1 Fat

Ricotta Cheese and Blueberry Parfait

no-bake **desserts**

Frozen Chocolate-Covered Bananas

Makes 4 servings

>2 ripe medium bananas
>4 wooden sticks
>½ cup low-fat granola cereal without raisins
>⅓ cup hot fudge topping, at room temperature

1. Line baking sheet or 15×10-inch jelly-roll pan with waxed paper; set aside.

2. Peel bananas; cut each in half crosswise. Insert wooden stick into center of cut end of each banana about 1½ inches into banana half. Place on prepared baking sheet; freeze until firm, at least 2 hours.

3. Place granola in large plastic food storage bag; crush slightly using rolling pin or meat mallet. Transfer granola to shallow plate. Place hot fudge topping in a shallow dish.

4. Working with one banana at a time, place frozen banana in hot fudge topping; turn banana and spread topping evenly onto banana with small rubber scraper. Immediately place banana on plate with granola; turn to coat lightly. Return to baking sheet in freezer. Repeat with remaining bananas.

5. Freeze until hot fudge topping is very firm, at least 2 hours. Place on small plates; let stand 5 minutes before serving.

Nutrients per serving: ½ banana
Calories: 191, **Calories from Fat:** 19%, **Total Fat:** 4g,
Saturated Fat: 2g, **Cholesterol:** 3mg, **Sodium:** 132mg,
Carbohydrate: 38g, **Fiber:** 3g, **Protein:** 3g

Dietary Exchange: 1½ Starch, 1 Fruit, ½ Fat

acknowledgments

The publisher would like to thank the companies and organizations listed below for the use of their recipes and photographs in this publication.

Almond Board of California

Equal® sweetener

Glucerna® is a registered trademark of Abbott Laboratories

The Hershey Company

SPLENDA® is a trademark of McNeil Nutritionals, LLC

The Sugar Association, Inc.

index